★ANGELLA★

BEAUTYCHEMIST

The Look Up Series #4

D1592496

ANGELLA

BEAUTY CHEMIST

Real Women in S.T.E.A.M.

Aubre Andrus

"FOR THE GIRLS WHO ALWAYS
DREAM ABOUT WHAT THEY'LL
BE ONE DAY." — AA

Published by Adjective Animal Publishing in Santa Monica, California.

Visit us online at adjectiveanimalpublishing.com.

Design: Alice Connew
Photography: Ariel Moore
Logos: Shay Merritté
Illustrations: Aubre Andrus

6, 24 and 54, Paper clip illustration: Designed by rawpixel.com/Freepik; 6, 24 and 54,
Polaroid: Roland Deason/Unsplash; 9, Periodic table: OntheRunPhoto/iStock; 10, New
York: Michael Discenza/Unsplash; 10, San Francisco: Remi Thorel/Unsplash; 15, Waterfall:
Ben Guerin/Unsplash; 21, Pink beach: Patrick Ryan/Unsplash; 21, Pink clouds: Andrea
Ferrario/Unsplash; 21, Flamingos: Stephane Yaich/Unsplash; 21, Succulent: Erol Ahmed/
Unsplash; 21, Melon hearts: Brooke Lark/Unsplash; 21, Makeup brush: Amy Shamblen/
Unsplash; 21, Hibiscus: Jessica Sloan/Unsplash; 21, Mangoes: Mitchell Luo/Unsplash;
21, Lilies: Ethan Robertson/Unsplash; 21, Woman: Dom Aguiar/Unsplash; 28, University
of Calfornia-Davis campus: Nischal Malla/Unsplash; 28, Peter A. Rock Hall, Steven Tyler
PJs/Flickr; 31, Diamond: Tahlia Doyle/Unsplash; 35, Bootlace seed pods: Bernard Dupont/
Wikimedia; 43, Oil dropper: Enecta/Unsplash

Special thanks to Steven and Amanda Mason of Mason and Co. Global Lab.

Library of Congress Cataloging-in-Publication Data is available upon request.

ISBN 9781639460151 (paperback)
ISBN 9781639460168 (hardcover)
ISBN 9781639460175 (e-book)

TABLE OF CONTENTS

Angella ♡*

CHAPTER 1
MEET ANGELLA

LOTIONS, POTIONS, AND MORE!

A bath bomb hits the water. It begins to fizz and turn the water purple. It smells sweet like a flower. Have you ever wondered why that happens—and how? I can tell you!

I'm Angella, and I'm a chemist at a beauty company. I mix ingredients and turn them into products that people can use on their bodies like lotion, shampoo, bubble bath, nail polish, face wash, sunscreen, toothpaste, and more.

In order to make a beauty product, I have to know exactly what certain ingredients do and WHAT HAPPENS when they get mixed together. I also think about how a product will smell, look, feel, and perform.

Chemists spend a lot of time working in laboratories. A lab is a place where scientists can do research and perform experiments. That's how I learned which ingredients to combine in order to cause that fizzing reaction that a bath bomb makes when it mixes with water. Chemistry is a very **HANDS-ON** science.

A scientist who runs experiments in a lab is similar to a chef who creates new recipes in a kitchen. Both of us are mixing ingredients to see what will happen. **That means cooking is chemistry, too.**

You can often find me in my kitchen experimenting with different flavors and spices instead of following a recipe. I've memorized how certain foods and spices react in a pan. That allows me to explore different FLAVOR combinations. I'm a scientist after all!

Chemistry is the study of elements and how they change when they are combined. Everything in the world is made from elements. That means **chemistry is all around you**—from the water you drink to the air you breathe to the food you eat!

I love that I can write down a formula on paper that shows how elements will react with one another then I can go to the lab and actually make it happen. That's the best way to learn how elements combine with one another—it takes practice!

FUN FACT!

There are 118 chemical elements. That means everything in the world is made up of one or more of these elements.

I love seeing the products I've made on shelves at stores. I know people use my products **EVERY DAY**, which is so cool. Most importantly, my products can make people healthier and happier—and that makes me happy, too!

For example, I've created acne products that help teens and adults clear up their skin and feel more confident. I've made lotions that hydrate dry, itchy skin and make people feel more comfortable. When I learn that my product really works for someone, I feel GREAT.

It fills my heart when I can bring some kind of wellness, improvement, or joy to someone's life. I go to work every day knowing that **I can make a positive impact on people**. It's so satisfying! I'm lucky to have a job that is so fulfilling.

ALL ABOUT ANGELLA

I'm from...
New York

But now I live in...
San Francisco, CA

Summer or winter?
Winter—but only in California!

Birthday: June 2

Siblings: Two younger brothers

Pets: When I was younger, we had two dogs named Leela and Lola

ANGELLA'S FAVORITES

Color:
Pink

Food:
Kale and quinoa—anything healthy and vegetarian!

Place:
New York, New York and Florianopolis, Brazil

Sport:
Even though I've never played, I'm a big tennis fan!

Ice Cream Flavor:
Cookie dough

Chocolate or Vanilla?
Chocolate

Singing or Dancing?
Dancing

TV or Movies?
Movies

What is your favorite thing about yourself?

I like to think that I am open-minded and well-rounded. I'm also very driven and love to learn new things.

Does anything scare you?

I am scared of heights even though I've flown all over the world. I'm also afraid of public speaking, but that is something that gets better with practice.

Who do you look up to?

There are so many! My family and friends are always an inspiration. In the world of beauty, I look up to world-famous makeup artists like Pat McGrath.

What makes you unique?

I grew up in a multicultural family with different backgrounds, interests, and experiences. Growing up, my brothers and I were always exposed to people of all cultures through travel and family gatherings. I really enjoy learning about people from all over the world.

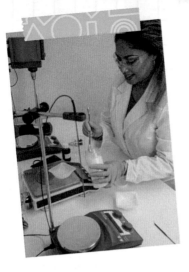

CHAPTER 2
HOW BEAUTY PRODUCTS GET MADE

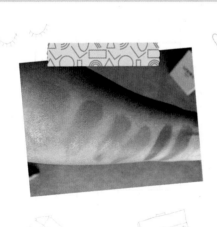

ꙮ FORMULA FUN ꙮ

When I want to create a new beauty product, the first thing I do is grab a **paper and pencil**. I need a concept, which is an idea for a product. I have to define exactly what that product will look like, feel like, smell like, and how it will perform.

Let's say I want to make a bath bomb. I might want it to smell like lavender and look bright purple in color. I want it to feel firm and solid in my hand, but then dissolve once it hits the water. I want it to F I Z Z—but not too fast! These are my expectations, or how I believe the product will look, feel, and behave.

Now I need to select my ingredients. On paper, I write down a list of ingredients and a ratio, or how much of each ingredient I will use. This is the formula, which is like the recipe for the product. I have memorized a basic starting formula for a lot of different beauty products thanks to all of the time I've spent in a lab. For example, I know I'll need a starch and an acid for a bath bomb.

My lab is filled with bottles, containers, and bags of different ingredients that I've purchased. They are filled with powder, liquid, wax, and gel forms of different chemicals. Before these chemicals were sold to chemists like me, they were either found in nature or made in a lab.

If a chemical was found in plants or a mineral from the earth, it's considered **NATURAL**. (There are also natural ingredients derived from animals, but I do not use those.) If it was made in a lab, it's called **SYNTHETIC**. Neither is necessarily better or worse.

Some beauty products are made from a mix of both natural and synthetic ingredients. And some lab-made ingredients come from nature. For example, coconuts have natural cleansing properties. A lab can **remove the cleansing chemicals** from the coconut then sell the coconut-based cleansing chemical to chemists like me.

SAVING SHARKS WITH SCIENCE

Chemists can make discoveries that make a huge difference. For example, squalane is a popular beauty ingredient that can help soften skin. Its natural form is found in shark liver oil. But chemists figured out how to recreate squalane in a lab using chemicals found in sugarcane plants. Even though it's made in a lab, it's the exact same chemical. Now, beauty products can be made with squalane and no sharks are harmed in the process.

H₂O = WATER!

Pick up a shampoo bottle and see what ingredient is listed on top—it's most likely water. Labels on beauty products list the ingredients in order from most to least. Many creams, lotions, shampoos, and conditioners are about sixty percent water.

Atoms are the small particles that elements are made of. The chemical elements that make up water are hydrogen and oxygen. When two hydrogen atoms and one oxygen atom join together, they form a water molecule. A molecule is two or more atoms that are joined together.

Water molecules help spread out all of the other ingredients evenly throughout the bottle. Water is good at dissolving other kinds of molecules, which is why products like shampoo and body wash easily rinse away in the bath or shower.

ℓ TO THE LAB! ℓ

Now it's time to head to the lab to test out my formula. I put on my white lab coat, tie my hair back, put on my safety goggles, and slip into some safety gloves. I weigh or measure my ingredients, mix them together, and see what happens. I use beakers, a scale, spatulas, a thermometer, a mixer, and a microscope. I might even heat or cool some ingredients.

I make many observations in the lab, which means I watch closely as I test my formula and take notes. **It's very matter of fact.** *Is my formula thick enough? Were my ratios slightly off?* I don't get disappointed or frustrated. I just observe. *Hmm, that didn't work. Let's make a small change to try to improve it.* I want the formula to match my expectations, and that might take many tries.

Once the formula is looking, feeling, and performing like it should, I pour it into a container and observe the final product. Being a beauty chemist means I have to find a **BALANCE** between the science and the artistic side.

Of course the product has to work. But I also consider the texture, color, and smell.

People don't use a product just because it works. They also use a product because it makes them feel really good, it looks beautiful, and it smells amazing. So, a bath bomb shouldn't just fizz and turn the bathwater a different color… it needs to do even more! A scent can make a big difference.

I know exactly what many different flowers smell like from geraniums to roses. I also know citrus scents like orange and grapefruit and herbal scents like lavender and rosemary. Usually, I have an idea of what I want my product to SMELL like, but I'll test my formula with a few different fragrances.

Next, I'll do a blind test with ten or more people to see which scent they like most. They'll smell product A, product B, and product C, but I won't tell them exactly what each formula is scented with. I'll narrow it down to two fragrances and then choose my favorite.

SMELLS GOOD!

Companies called fragrance houses develop scents for beauty products. It's their job to bottle up amazing smells. Some scents are taken from plants and flowers while others are recreated in a lab. They are sold as oils that chemists can add to their creations.

THE FINISHING TOUCHES

Something I also have to think about when I develop a product is how much my ingredients cost. Sometimes I love the smell of a certain fragrance, but it would make my product too expensive. I have a budget, which is **a certain amount of money I can spend**. I know exactly how much certain ingredients cost and how well they work—so I know if they are worth the extra price.

Once I have my formula perfected with the perfect scent, it's my job as the chemist to recommend a package. The ingredients determine which kind of package we can use. For example, if a formula is made with highly acidic ingredients, then it can't go in a plastic bottle. **The acid will break down the plastic bottle over time.** It will have to go in a glass container instead.

I'll also recommend how the product should be dispensed. For example, should that lotion go in a squeeze bottle or a pump bottle? Or maybe a jar is better? We'll select two or three different packages based on my recommendations. Even though the formula is complete, there is still a lot of testing that needs to be done.

First, we'll ask real people to test out the product in the package. We ask them how well the product worked, if they liked it, and what they would change. We are always curious what **REAL PEOPLE** are looking for in their beauty products.

We also send the packaged product to a special safety lab to make sure the formula doesn't grow mold over time. **Yuck!** We also do stability testing, which means we heat the formula in an oven, cool it in a refrigerator, freeze it then thaw it, and observe it at room temperature.

The product will likely be delivered in all kinds of weather to various stores around the country and then kept in people's homes. This testing recreates any kind of stress the product might be put under.

We test the formula in both a glass container and in the recommended package to see how it reacts. We do this over the course of **THREE TO SIX MONTHS!** We make sure the package doesn't break down, that the formula doesn't change color, and that the ingredients don't start separating from each other.

What if they do? Then it's time to test a new package—or a new formula! For example, I've learned one month into testing that one of my natural formulas started **CHANGING COLORS**. There are so many things that can happen along the way.

But if everything goes well, I work with a production lab that can turn one small product into five hundred products, ten thousand products, or maybe even fifty thousand products! **First, they'll make a small batch of products**. They give me samples from the small batch to approve. If they look and feel just like my original formula, then it's time for full-scale production.

It's ʃO COOL to watch beauty products get made in a manufacturing plant. There are huge drums that dispense the formula into bottles. Each bottle is filled, labeled, put in a small box, grouped into large boxes, then sent to a warehouse where it will eventually be shipped to stores. Then it gets purchased and used by people like you!

MOOD BOARD

Sometimes I pin different images, textures, and colors to a bulletin board for inspiration when I'm creating a new product. Maybe I want something to be pink, but do I want it to be a dusty pink or a bright fuschia pink? These mood boards can help me decide.

FROM IDEA TO BEAUTY PRODUCT

1. The product starts with a concept. It's a description of the product from what it looks like to how it will perform.

2. Next, chemists develop the formula, which is the list of ingredients and how much of each ingredient will be used. It's like the recipe for the product.

3. Chemists test the formula in a lab, make observations, and tweak the formula until it meets the expectations of the concept.

4. We make sure the ingredients fit into our budget, or the amount of money we can spend, on this product.

8. Now it's time to turn one product into many! We send the formula to a production lab to make a batch of production samples. These products are an exact replica of our original formula.

7. In stability testing, chemists heat, freeze, and thaw the product to make sure it doesn't change colors or separate. This takes three to six months.

9. Once we've approved the samples, thousands more products can be made in a manufacturing plant. The formula is poured into bottles, wrapped with labels, and packaged into boxes.

6. The product heads to a safety testing lab to make sure it won't grow mold in the packaging.

10. The beauty products are shipped to warehouses then stores where they can be purchased by people around the country!

5. Based on the ingredients, chemists make a recommendation for how to package the product. Glass or plastic? Pump or squeeze bottle?

FUN FACT!

It takes 9 months to 2 years (or more) for a beauty product to be created, depending on how much research is needed.

Happy 6th birthday to me!

I ♡ CHEMISTRY

CHAPTER 3
HOW DID I GET HERE?

SCIENCE

SCHOOL DAYS

I wasn't interested in science as a kid. I never did science kits or experiments in my kitchen. But I did love animals from reptiles to horses to dogs. Of all the sciences, you'd think I would have been drawn to **biology or zoology**. Nothing really pointed me to chemistry as a kid.

My absolute favorite game to play was chess. Honestly, I loved anything that involved solving problems like puzzle cubes that you had to spin and spin until the colors on all sides lined up. My mom also signed me up for piano and violin. **MUSIC HELPED WITH MY CREATIVITY** and forced me to expand my mind into different ways of thinking.

In school, I always did better in the more artistic classes like music, Spanish, art, and writing. Those classes always felt easy to me while science and math were much more challenging. **Even though I didn't always do well, I liked them anyway.** Science in particular always kept me interested.

I grew up in New York. My dad's family is from the U.S. Virgin Islands and my mom's side of the family is Guyanese. Guyana is a small country in South America next to Venezuela. It's considered a Caribbean country and is a very natural and untouched place with lush rainforests and beautiful waterfalls.

Because my mom grew up in Guyana around so many plants and flowers in the rainforest, she always had some kind of plant remedy for us when something went wrong. For example, when I was young, we used to break off pieces of an aloe plant and put the gel from inside the leaf on our face. **It feels really cool and relaxing!** Plants were such a big part of our everyday health.

As a kid, I realized that there was some kind of special chemistry that could be released from plants and that they could offer a lot of BENEFITS to people. But I never knew that I could one day turn that knowledge into a career.

In high school, I liked science enough that I decided I should be a doctor one day. The truth is that I didn't know what other kinds of careers you could have if you liked science. But I was very driven and excited about the idea of college.

So much so that I wanted to finish high school early.

I started taking night classes so I could graduate a year early from high school. I had already skipped a grade in elementary school, so this wasn't new to me. **WHEN I STARTED COLLEGE, I WAS ONLY 16!** I was pre-med, which meant that I wanted to go to medical school and become a doctor one day.

During my first year of college, I had to take a ton of science classes—and I failed all of them. I got a D or an F in every one! However, I got As in all the creative classes. I knew something was wrong. **Science wasn't clicking for me, but I still loved it.** I needed to take a break and figure out what was best for me.

School: University of California-Davis
Location: Davis, California
Major: Chemistry

The Univeristy of California-Davis has a big campus!

The second largest lecture hall at UC-Davis is in the Chemistry building.

PETER A. ROCK HALL

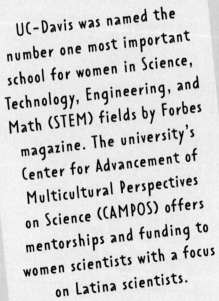

UC-Davis was named the number one most important school for women in Science, Technology, Engineering, and Math (STEM) fields by Forbes magazine. The university's Center for Advancement of Multicultural Perspectives on Science (CAMPOS) offers mentorships and funding to women scientists with a focus on Latina scientists.

OFF TO UNIVERSITY!

I didn't want to give up on college or science, so I transferred to a new school: the University of California-Davis. It was all the way across the country in northern California. I had to re-take all of the classes that I failed. One of those classes was chemistry. But the teacher made me look at chemistry in a **TOTALLY NEW WAY**.

Teachers in college are called professors. The professor made chemistry real for me. It was the first time I realized that even the water we drink is chemistry. Everything is chemistry! Before this, I had only seen chemistry written in a book or on the whiteboard. It didn't feel relatable to my life. But now it did!

Finally, chemistry really clicked for me. I decided that I didn't want to be a doctor anymore. I wanted to be a chemistry major. **I focused all my time and effort on chemistry.** After class, I'd test out things I had just learned. For example, after learning about acids and bases, I tried dissolving the soap scum on my bathtub ledge with vinegar—it worked!

As a chemistry major, I spent a lot of time in the lab with my classmates during college. Sometimes we partnered up and sometimes we worked alone. This was so helpful for me because **I could really see with my own two eyes what we had just learned in the classroom**. I loved that chemical reactions didn't just happen on paper or in a book. I could make things happen in real life.

STAYING SAFE IN THE LAB

When you're dealing with the mixing and heating of chemicals, it's important to stay safe. We never want to accidentally start a fire, break a glass, or splash chemicals in our eyes. That's why we use safety goggles to protect our eyes, lab coats to protect our clothing, and heat-resistant gloves or tongs when picking up a hot test tube or beaker. Anyone with long hair should tie their hair back, too. I very carefully read all labels and safety data sheets that come with every chemical before mixing ingredients. I also make sure that the glass beakers or test tubes I'm using are fully cleaned and aren't chipped. Safety first!

I learned so much in my classes, but I wanted to learn even more. On my own time, I started researching and applying to extra chemistry programs at other colleges. Sometimes colleges offer week-long or summer-long research programs for students from other schools.

I got to study in a DIAMOND LAB at Arizona State University for a week. They literally make diamonds in a lab! I thought that was so, so cool. That's when I started to realize that I was meant for chemistry. I wasn't sure what I wanted to do with my degree yet, but I knew that **I could always grow diamonds!**

Then I did a summer research program at Northwestern University in Illinois. Finally, I spent my whole senior year back at UC-Davis doing research about why and how some chemicals are magnetic while others aren't. Some of my research was even **PUBLISHED IN SCIENTIFIC JOURNALS**, which usually doesn't happen when you're still in college. I really was doing everything I could to learn everything I could about chemistry.

WHAT IS COLLEGE?

Angella has a degree in chemistry. Here's what that means and why she earned it.

Angella went to college for four years after high school. In order to go to college, you must apply and get accepted. Good grades, after-school activities, volunteer experience, and letters of recommendation from teachers or community members can help you get accepted into a university.

People go to college to learn more about a specific career like chemistry. After four years, if you've passed all of your classes, you get an undergraduate degree like Angella did. It's a certificate that proves that you know a lot about a certain subject. Knowing a lot about a certain subject can help you find a good job.

WHAT IS
A JOB?

Angella's job is 'cosmetic chemist.' Why do people like Angella have a job?

People work at a job in order to make money, which can be used to pay for a place to live, food, clothing, and fun things like travel and entertainment. Jobs give people a sense of purpose, or a reason to use their talents every day. Jobs can also make the world a better place by helping other people or by solving big problems. You can meet cool people and learn new things at a job.

Have you ever made money by doing a chore or task?

What are some careers that you can think of?

What kind of jobs do the people in your life have?

CHAPTER 4
BEAUTY EVERYWHERE

totally natural.
Super good.
Absolutely beautiful.

ℓ NATURAL BEAUTY ℓ

Taking care of yourself is very important. It's something I do every day. And it's part of the reason why I enjoy making beauty products so much. I've made all different kinds of products for many different companies, but now I run my own beauty brand. And it's INSPIRED by Guyana.

Thanks to my mom, I've always loved how plants, flowers, and tea leaves could make us look and feel good. There is one ingredient that my mom loves called **bootlace tree extract.** In Guyana, locals use resin and oil from the bootlace tree bark to heal toothaches and wounds. But it's also been proven to be **REALLY GOOD FOR SKIN.**

These are seed pods on a bootlace tree!

When I make beauty products, I like to use chemicals that have been collected from plants because plants are easily regrown, which means they are a SUSTAINABLE ingredient. Plants can even provide natural coloring. Flower petals and dried beets can be turned into pretty pink powders when crushed. I think it's really cool that so many powerful ingredients can be found in nature.

One day at a trade show, I saw that bootlace tree extract was now being sold as an ingredient. I couldn't believe it. I could buy this ingredient right now and start making beauty products with it. I knew I had to start a company that featured **natural ingredients from the Guyanese rainforest.** It was meant to be!

Starting my own company was just another way that I pushed myself to become a better chemist. It was scary at first, but now I'm so glad that I did it. I'm so PROUD of the products I've created including lotions, face oils, bar soaps, and teas. I'm making people healthier and happier with my products but I'm also bringing attention to the beautiful country of Guyana.

I'm always researching new plant-based ingredients. I only want to use ingredients that really work and are safe. It's my job as a chemist to read and understand the data and the testing behind each ingredient, as well as learn how the ingredient was made. Chemistry is so cool because **there are always new innovations**, which are new discoveries and ideas. I'm always learning, experimenting, and growing as a beauty chemist. I wouldn't want it any other way!

COOL CHEMISTRY

Scientists are always developing amazing new ingredients for beauty products. When I go to trade shows and read trade publications, which are meetings and magazines for people who work in a certain career, I get to learn about the latest discoveries. I also love walking through the beauty sections of stores, too, and admiring all the new products.

GLITTER AND GLOW

If a beauty product is glittery or shimmery, that means the formula is reflective—like a mirror. A sparkly mineral used to be mixed into lotions or nail polish to add shimmer. But now scientists make a synthetic version in a lab. The particles are larger and smoother so they reflect light even better like a prism.

FIZZING FUN

Bath bombs are often made by combining baking soda and citric acid. When those ingredients are placed in water, a chemical reaction occurs. The ingredients begin to dissolve into the water and it makes a lot of bubbles, which is actually carbon dioxide gas being released. That's the fizz!

TEMPORARY COLOR

If you've ever put a streak of color in your hair just for fun, you've seen some color chemistry. Small pigment molecules (pigment is another word for color) attach to the outside of each individual piece of hair. The molecules will eventually get removed by shampoo and water.

∼ INNER BEAUTY ∼

I love chemistry but it's not all that I do. Another way I take care of myself is by moving my body and calming my mind. Plus, I've found that having interests outside of work actually makes my work more interesting.

I love going to yoga classes after work and on the weekends. In yoga class, I do a series of quiet poses, stretches, and breathing. It keeps me GROUNDED AND FEELING PEACEFUL. I've been practicing yoga for twenty years!

More recently, I've tried something **TOTALLY DIFFERENT**—I started Latin dancing! I had never taken a dance class as a kid and I would not call myself athletic. But I signed up anyway. I especially like the samba, which is a really energetic, upbeat dance that's popular in Brazil.

Dancing the samba is a very different way of moving my body and pushing my body. I love it! I feel great when I learn a new move that I never would have been able to do three years ago. I've even traveled to Rio de Janeiro, Brazil to dance with my friends at Carnival. It's a huge celebration with lots of sparkly costumes and samba dancing in the streets. It was amazing!

When I first started in science, I felt like I didn't quite fit in. I had a degree in chemistry, I loved it, but I really didn't know where it would take me. There weren't many other chemists that looked like me or had the same interests as me.

But I always stayed focused on the job at hand. I knew I was smart and that **my voice deserved to be heard**. It helped that I studied really hard and really understood all sides of chemistry. Now I know that I'm right where I'm supposed to be. It took me a bit of time to find my way, but I got here!

There are so many different kinds of companies you can work for if you have a science degree. Don't feel limited by traditional science careers. **You can always find a job that connects with your passion.** For me, it was beauty products. For you, it might be something else. Just be yourself, follow your passions, and see where they lead. You never know where life will take you!

ANGELLA'S ADVICE FOR YOUNG CHEMISTS

ALWAYS BE YOURSELF.

Just be you. What you love will come to you naturally and then you will automatically want to work hard at it.

DON'T GIVE UP.

When you know what you like, stick with it. Even if you are unsure where it will lead, know that something good will come out of it. There is a place for you somewhere!

TAKE CHARGE.

I went out of my way to learn everything I could about chemistry. I signed up for extra programs on my own, asked professors if they needed help with research, and more. Go the extra distance. You'll learn more about yourself, too.

SCIENCE IS FOR EVERYONE.

The world of science is vast! There are so many things you can do with a degree in science, and so many different paths it can lead you on. Science might fit right in with one of your passion whether it's working with animals, helping others, or making cool beauty products.

YOU CAN ALWAYS LEARN A NEW SKILL.

When it comes to science, there is so much to learn, which is really exciting. Don't get discouraged if you don't pick up on something right away. Ask someone to explain it to you in a new way until it sticks.

CHAPTER 5
YOU CAN BE A
BEAUTY CHEMIST

SEE IT, SMELL IT, FEEL IT

A beauty chemist has to know how certain ingredients feel, smell, perform, and what they look like. Here are some ingredients you can get to know in your own home.

OILS

If you have any of these oils at home in your kitchen, rub a small amount onto the back of your hand to see how they smell, look, and feel. Which one do you prefer?

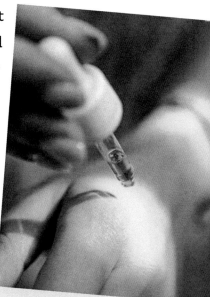

- OLIVE OIL
- COCONUT OIL
- VEGETABLE OIL
- AVOCADO OIL

BODY OF WATER

Your skin is made up of sixty four percent water. Your skin naturally makes oils to lock in this water, so that it won't get dry and flaky. Adding more oil on top of your skin can help. Oils like olive oil have healthy fats and vitamins that can help moisturize your skin and help repair your skin.

SCENTS

Certain fragrances are popular in beauty products. If you have any of these herbs, fruits, or ingredients in your home, give them a sniff and decide which ones are your favorite. Do any pair well together?

CITRUS SCENTS: Ask an adult to cut open a fresh lemon, orange, or grapefruit. Can you close your eyes and identify all three by scent alone?

HERBAL SCENTS: Rosemary, mint, and lavender are popular herbal flavors that you can find as dried spices, fresh at the grocery store, or within tea leaves.

FLORAL SCENTS: Jasmine, rose, and chamomile are common floral scents that you may be able to find in tea leaves or essential oils.

BAKERY SCENTS: Vanilla extract, brown sugar, and cocoa (from cocoa powder) are also popular scents for beauty products that might be found in your kitchen cabinet.

SUPER SMELLS

Scientists have found that certain smells, like lavender and jasmine, can be very soothing. They can even lower stress and are proven to help you feel more calm. What scents make you feel more calm? How do each of the scents above make you feel?

Which oils did you like most?

Which ones didn't you like and why?

Which fragrances did you like most?

Which ones didn't you like and why?

OIL AND WATER

Beauty chemists love using oils. They are really moisturizing for the skin. When you moisturize your skin, it means that your skin will be able to better absorb water, which makes your skin less dry. However, there's one big problem. Most beauty products are water-based. And oil and water don't mix. So what's a beauty chemist to do? An experiment, of course!

TRY IT YOURSELF!

Pour 1/4 cup olive oil and 1/4 cup water into a glass. Observe for 30 seconds. What happens? (Save the cup for an experiment on the next page.)

Write down your observations here.

FUN FACT!

Experiments like this are exactly how Angella learned different chemistry concepts and memorized how different ingredients behave.

The only way to mix oil and water is by adding an emulsifier to the formula. An emulsifier helps spread little droplets of oil evenly throughout the water-based formula. It allows beauty chemists to add moisturizing oils to water-based lotions.

Emulsifiers are used in cooking, too. Mayonnaise is one example of oil and water mixing together with help from an emulsifier. What's the secret emulsifier in mayonnaise? It's egg yolk! Let's see what happens when we add an egg yolk to our oil and water mix.

Write down your observations here.

TRY IT YOURSELF!

Pour the oil and water mixture from the previous page into a bowl. Crack an egg into a second small bowl and use the shell to scoop out just the yolk (the yellow part). Drop the yolk into the oil and water mixture. Using a whisk, blend the mix together for 15 seconds. Pour it back into the cup and observe. What happens?

～ FACE MASK ～

A wash-off face mask is relaxing to wear and makes your skin extra soft. Many ingredients in your kitchen offer natural benefits for skin. One example is avocados, which are made of healthy fats and vitamins that help moisturize your skin.

One way to make a formula moisturizing is by adding a humectant. It's an ingredient that draws water toward your skin like a magnet. Honey is a natural humectant. When you combine avocado, honey, and oatmeal, which helps calm skin, you've created the perfect face mask.

Make your own face mask by following these steps:

YOU WILL NEED:

- 1 cup old fashioned oats
- ½ avocado
- 1 tbsp honey
- 1 tbsp olive oil
- Blender
- Spatula
- Small bowl

TO MAKE:

1. Add all ingredients to a blender.

2. Mix well until smooth.

3. Pour into a bowl. You may need a spatula to scoop everything out of the blender.

TO USE:

1. Gently apply a thin layer of mixture to your face with your fingers then wash your hands.

2. Wear the mask for up to 15 minutes. You may want to lay down on a couch or bed as it dries.

3. Rinse off over the kitchen sink and pat dry with a clean washcloth.

4. Discard the extras in the trash.

Write down any observations about the formula here. What did you like or not like? How would you improve it? Does your skin look or feel different?

ℯ LIP SCRUB ℯ

Angella scrubs her lips with this mixture to make them feel super soft. This process is called exfoliation. When you exfoliate, you remove a layer of old, dry skin and reveal newer, softer skin below. Did you know your body is always creating new skin cells and shedding old ones?

Make your own lip scrub by following these steps:

YOU WILL NEED:

- 1 ½ tbsp liquid coconut oil*
  or olive oil
- 2 tbsp white sugar
- 1 tbsp brown sugar

HERE'S A TIP!

Don't exfoliate too often! Once a week is enough. You can use this scrub as a hand scrub, too.

*liquid coconut oil can be found at grocery or health food stores.

TO MAKE:

1. Add ingredients to a small bowl. Mix well.

2. Pour into a small, lidded glass jar.

3. Store in the refrigerator until you're ready to use. This mix should be used within 1 to 2 weeks.

TO USE:

1. When you're ready to use, dip a spoon into the jar and scoop a small amount onto your fingers.

2. Rub your fingers together to warm up the mix, then rub it onto your lips.

3. Keep scrubbing for 15 seconds then rinse your lips over the sink with a wet washcloth.

Write down any observations about the formula here. What did you like or not like? How would you improve it? Do your lips look or feel different?

✒ FOOT SCRUB ✑

Like sugar, salt is also a natural exfoliant. And it's actually really good for your skin. When rubbed on your feet, salt can help get rid of dry skin patches and soften your skin.

Make your own foot scrub by following these steps:

YOU WILL NEED:

- ¼ cup of liquid coconut oil*
- 1 cup of salt
- ½ cup vegetable oil like olive oil
- Optional: 2 to 5 drops of peppermint essential oil*
- Small bowl
- Large bowl
- Spoon

Fine-grain salt or course-grain salt will work in this scrub. Fine-grain salt will make for a softer scrub, while coarse-grain salt will make for a rougher scrub. You can use this mixture as a hand scrub, too.

*liquid coconut oil and essential oils can be found at grocery or health food stores.

TO MAKE:

- Add all the ingredients to a small bowl.

- Mix well with a spoon until the oils and salt are blended well.

TO USE:

1. Place a towel on the bathroom floor.

2. Fill a large bowl less than halfway with warm water and set it on top of the towel. Submerge one foot into the bowl.

3. Scoop a handful of scrub onto your wet foot and begin massaging it into your foot for 30 seconds.

4. Rinse your foot in the bowl, then dry it completely with a dry towel.

5. Repeat with the other foot.

6. Dispose of extra water and scrub in the sink.

Write down any observations about the formula here. What did you like or not like? How would you improve it? Do your feet look or feel different?

Here I am traveling around
the city for work!

CHAPTER 6
LOOK UP!

WHY WE LOOK UP TO ANGELLA

SHE'S DRIVEN.

Angella has always reached for the stars. She goes above and beyond in order to achieve everything she possibly can.

SHE'S INVENTIVE.

Scientists can be creative, too. Angella is always researching and brainstorming new ways to use ingredients, colors, scents, textures, and more.

SHE'S CARING.

Her job may be to create products in a lab, but Angella's main goal is always to bring happiness and wellness to others.

SHE'S RESOURCEFUL.

Angella's curiosity drove her to learn everything she could about chemistry. When she hit a roadblock, she tried again until she found her way.

SHE'S CONFIDENT.

Angella knows she's an asset, which means her voice and her skills are needed and important. She's never shied away from an opportunity even if she was a little scared at first.

I'd love to learn everything there is to know about ...

Can you think of a time that you failed, but tried again?

In what ways are you inventive?

What hobbies and activities do you love doing after school?

Talk about a time you felt very confident.

Describe a time you learned a new skill and were really proud.

↵ LOOK UP MORE! ↵

If any of the topics in this book inspired you, head to the library to find more information or ask an adult to help you search online. Here are some ideas to get you started.

CHEMISTRY

The Exploratorium, a museum in San Francisco (where Angella lives), shares tons of interesting chemistry experiments on their website:

exploratorium.edu/snacks/subject/chemistry

YOGA

You can increase your flexibility, strength, and mindfulness by practicing some new yoga moves at the Cosmic Kids YouTube channel: **youtube.com/cosmickidsyoga**

BATH AND BODY

Science Buddies shares science fair project ideas from bath bombs to make-your-own shampoo:

sciencebuddies.org/science-fair-projects/project-ideas/cosmetic-chemistry

ABOUT THE EXPERT

Angella Sprauve is a Formulation Chemist and Product Development Consultant specializing in clean beauty innovation. As a chemistry graduate from University of California-Davis, she began her career as a Cosmetic Chemist then continued into New Product Development to lead skincare, haircare, and color cosmetic innovation for clean beauty leaders such as Yes to Carrots and Juice Beauty. She is experienced working with emerging indie brands and big box beauty brands. For more, visit **angellasprauve.com**.

ABOUT THE AUTHOR

Aubre Andrus is an award-winning children's book author with dozens of books published by American Girl, National Geographic Kids, Lonely Planet Kids, Disney, Scholastic, and more. Her titles encourage kids to be kind and be curious, and she is committed to writing books that empower girls and inspire them to become the leaders of tomorrow. Aubre received her degree in journalism and film from the University of Wisconsin. She currently lives in Los Angeles with her husband and daughter. For more, visit **aubreandrus.com**.

WHO'S NEXT?

Meet Tracey, a theme park designer who proves just how scientific art can be. Tracey struggled with numbers as a kid, but now she uses her unique way of thinking to turn art into experiences that families around the world love.

Meet Dr. Maya, a food scientist who believes ice cream can change the world. Maya does what she loves, which is traveling the globe, developing delicious flavors, and sharing her love of science with everyone.

Parents and educators, visit **thelookupseries.com** to see who you can meet next and to find video interviews, free downloads, and more.

Made in the USA
Monee, IL
04 December 2022

19392254R10038